Echos of Resilience

Amanda Smith

BookLeaf Publishing

India | USA | UK

Presentation by *BookLeaf Publishing*

Web: www.bookleafpub.com

E-mail: info@bookleafpub.com

ISBN: 9789360943448

First edition 2024

Dedicated to my incredible parents – Mom, you're the reason for my heartbeat and the unwavering force behind every step I take. Dad, though you're no longer physically here, your legacy lives on in every breath. This book exists because you both believed in my dreams and had my back through thick and thin. You're not just the roots; you're the reason I reach for the stars. In every word, you'll find the echoes of your love, the reason I'm alive and thriving. Forever grateful for your presence in my life.

ACKNOWLEDGEMENT

In the grand symphony of life, I want to turn up the volume on gratitude to those who made this book possible. Massive shoutout to my ride-or-die fam, you're the real MVPs. Big ups to my squad, your vibes kept me going. To the little legends in my life, your boundless energy is my daily boost. And to my love, you're the anchor in my chaotic seas. This project wouldn't have been the same without your vibes, love, and mad support. Here's to the crew that lights up my world – you rock!

PREFACE

Hey friend,

Embarking on the pages of this book is not just a literary journey but a shared exploration of resilience, triumph, and the intricate dance of the human experience. In these words, I invite you to immerse yourself in the essence of what follows—a collection of poems that unveil the depths of my heart and the echoes of resilience that have shaped my life. As I write this preface, I am reminded that every journey begins with a first step, and I am grateful that you have chosen to take this step with me.

In the wreckage

In the wreckage of trauma's grasp,
Marks linger, memories clasp.
Safe, yet scarred, I fled the past,
Escape the remedy, freedom amassed.

Hostile hands, shattered plans,
Broken, but hope still withstands.
In something new, a future unfolds,
A story of resilience, as life molds.

A haven anew, love's gentle touch,
Sent from above, a blessing as such.
He freed my soul from trauma's toll,
Made me whole, revived my soul.

Trauma's not defining, just a scar,
Once there, but now afar.
Far away from the pain I've known,
I'm okay, with a love that's grown.

Safety, love intertwined,
A rescue, a solace I find.
Saved by the one who set me free,
In their arms, I'm who I want to be.

Survivors Decree

In the chaos of a flipped car's chance,
I emerged unscathed, given a glance.
Life's lens shifted, colors anew,
Grateful echoes, a profound view.

Four kiddos relying on my breath,
A mother's worry, a lover's depth.
Dodged the dog, avoided despair,
Fate suspended in the midair.

A brush with demise, a moment in time,
Frozen as the car rolled, a pantomime.
Breath held, submerged in life's cascade,
Drowned in memories that gently swayed.

Items suspended, mid-flight ballet,
A slow-motion reel of life at play.
I'm okay, a survivor's decree,
Resilient spirit, alive and free.

The Mojo In The Madness

I feel lucky through the chaos
Blessed through the storm
Life has a certain embrace now
Like I've never felt before

My truth is that there's more to my story
I have more goals I need to meet
For my family to acquire comfort and greatness
Verses disaster and defeat.

Your scars and trauma are just that
Glimpses of a tougher time that you prove you
can survive and take back what's yours
Take a breath, take a leap and say goodbye to
that curse

There's a mojo in the madness
That madness creates a soldier
A fortress of resilience
Even when you're older

In the serene stillness
After the storm passes and it's nothing but a soft
silence

The self assurance awakens the beauty of a soul
no longer trapped by traumas grasp and a new
journey begins.

Dad

In the quiet echoes of the past, I miss,
A father's hug, a tender reminisce.
His words, a melody like Pink Floyd's song,
A symphony of memories where we belong.

Sitting outside, beneath the open sky,
His presence felt as the days pass by.
Thanksgivings without him, a bittersweet grace,
His essence lingers, a cherished embrace.

Three years gone, yet his spirit stays,
Guiding me through life's intricate maze.
I yearn for his wisdom, his comforting voice,
In the silence, I long for his choice.

Holidays echo with the void he left,
His absence keenly felt, hearts bereft.
His cooking, a taste of love untold,
A culinary tale of memories to hold.

I miss him deeply, the laughter we'd share,
The bond unbroken, though he's not there.
In the tapestry of time, his love's woven,
A cherished presence, forever chosen.

** I miss you dad. Love you more**

Reality Breach

Here I am swaying,
Are my thoughts betraying?
My mind... I listen closely,
I can't focus on the least,
Important part of it solely.
Because I won't go far,
If I can't make it up to par,
Reality.

Taking chances on new things,
Because you listen to society.
Why can't I complete the task?
The end is on the other end,
Just about in sight of me.

Yet, a tinge of regret lingers,
For not achieving more,
But amid the sway, a shift in perspective,
A sense of accomplishment grows,
For being willing to change and explore.

Syncopate

Surrounded by the frequency of yesterday's
regrets,
On the cusp of a new choice, not my best choice
yet.
Leaving the old for the new, hoping it stays in
view,
Until the new becomes old news, regretting it
too.

I know the blessings born from choices
Don't have to make sense to you,
After all, it's me who's mother to the two.
My son and daughter, with who
We grew up together, forging a bond nothing can
alter.

Different versions of myself, yet intertwined,
In this journey where life's lessons are defined.
Now, as pillars of strength, you stand,
Extra support for your little sisters 6 and 1 in the
same band.

From the same womb, a legacy of love,
A familial tapestry woven from above.
Forever united, our story unfolds,
A narrative of growth, love, and bonds that hold.

Reflections of Resilience

A girl who promised and failed to keep it. You made plans, and now you sleep on it. You went to great lengths to try again, but you quit. You just don't try anymore. This isn't where your story ends. You can change the world if you want to, but that's all up to you believing in YOU!

Who are you?

Take that leap, brace for change. Love hard, hug longer, and don't stay the same. You have goals. What's stopping you? What's meant to be will surely come through.

Who is she?

Your past does not define you. You can do this if you try too. Don't be the girl you left behind. While she's still there, it's not her time. It's yours.

Matriarch of Resilience

Through countless battles and the hardships you
faced,
You not only saved yourself but also protected
us with grace.
It wasn't easy, every doubt overcome,
Building thick skin, a journey seldom won.

Always there, keeping us safe, clothed, and fed,
More than a mom, my best friend instead.
Pushing me forward when all seemed lost,
Never giving up, no matter the cost.

Through thick and thin, you stood by,
A beacon of strength, reaching the sky.
Not just a mother, but a beacon bright,
In your love, I find unyielding might.

I get it from her, you know,
The stubbornness and will to chase.
To handle my encounters, face to face.

I'll push through hardships, and protect my own,
Forever grateful to you, mom, until the end is
known.

Freedoms Embrace

Taken aback, yet moving forward,
In the quiet, I continue onward.
Leaving the pining in the past,
Overnight, I head towards the vast dawn.

Freely like the leaves flowing in the wind,
I aim to feel the same, free.
Freely like the waves, rapidly yet calmly,
Rippling in the sea.
Freely like the birds, out of formation,
All around.
Freely like the song I sing, oh how I love the
sound of freedom.

I don't wait for sadness; it leaves me to my own.
I hate to feel the anger and the pressure; I prefer
my zone.
I get to be in charge of my head now; my
freedom is how I know it.
And in my days to come, I know exactly how to
show it.

Freedom, freely, free,
Freedom freeing me.
Freedom flying forward, onward,

Freedom flying free.

Freedom freely free,
Freedom freeing me.
Freedom flying forward, onward,
Freedom flies through me.

I am finally free,
Just me,
Just free.

Synchronic Ties: Healing Through Chaos

In the shadows of heartbreak, where sorrow
holds sway,
A tale unfolds of friendships formed in the
disarray.
Through breakups and wild nights, our paths
converged,
Losing ourselves, in each other's tales fully
submerged.

Amidst the wreckage of love, we found a
common ground,
Connecting through music's solace, a healing
sound.
Endless talks under city lights, sharing our fears,
Building each other up, wiping away the tears.

Lost in the chaos of life's twists and turns,
We discovered solace in friendship as the fire
burns.
Putting pieces back together, like a mosaic of
grace,
Regardless of the fallout, the healing we
embrace.

Through the echoes of laughter and the silent
cries,
We navigated the storms, beneath urban skies.
In the tapestry of time, our bonds were spun,
An appreciation for the healing, for battles won.

So here's to the friendships that weather the
strife,
Born from the fragments of our shared life.
In the symphony of scars, a melody so
appealing,
For the friends who became the balm for each
feeling.

Storms Dance

I hear it falling swiftly,
Rain's pitter-patter, a rhythmic symphony.
Thunder dances with lightning's spark,
Wind clings to the unstable, waiting dark.

Tornado born, searching wide,
Everywhere, nowhere, it'll confide.
Found by victims, by chance, too late,
Disappears into the unpredictable state.

Thunder dies, lights extinguished,
Leaving behind a silence undistinguished.
All that lingers, the relentless soothing drops of
rain,
Pitter-patter, a timeless refrain.

The longing

In the silence of the night, I search for peace,
A river of solace, a longing release.
The end arrived too soon, not my decree,
Lost in the distance, burdening me.

Days stretch out, an endless line,
Nights linger longer, the ache is mine.
Heart heavy with sorrow, yet duty remains,
Little ones depend, their needs in chains.

You were needed, a presence profound,
Now, an absence, silence all around.
Aching heart, yet the job persists,
In the shadows, where your presence exists.

Peace, like the river's gentle flow,
Relief, a tale I yearn to know.
In the echoes of longing, where are you?
I navigate this path, steadfast and true.

Threads of Resilience

In the night's darkness,
And all the world's lights become the moon,
When quiet surrounds me,
Like a string on a loom.

When the air is cold,
And the world is asleep,
In my head again,
These thoughts they creep.

"You can't do it,
You won't make it,
You don't have what it takes.
You are broken,
You are shattered,
This is why your heart breaks."

In the midday while I'm driving,
While going to and from,
In the evening when I'm cooking,
Or cleaning before the day is done.

When needs are met,
When the kids are set,
When the daily things are done,

What happens when it's someone saying,

"You can't do it,
You won't make it,
You don't have what it takes.
You are broken,
You are shattered,
This is why your heart breaks."

Yet, in the shadows, a truth unfolds,
It's not their choice, but mine, to behold.
To feel better, to push ahead,
My strength, my will, by my own thread.

The Morning Worry

In the brisk morn, where goosebumps reside,
A journey unfolds, emotions as our guide.
Warmth blossoms through the day's embrace,
Mental strength prevailing, enveloped in grace.

Yet, as the night descends, cold returns,
Anxiety whispers, and worry burns.
Cycles repeat, a relentless tide,
But dawn brings hope, fears set aside.

In the dance of temperature and soul's sway,
A poem of resilience, day by day.

Kindred Threads: Family and Friends Weave the Fabric of Me

I have eyes like my mama, quick wit like my dad, hair like my grandma, hugs like granddad. Brave like my brother, a little lost like my sis. Parts of them are parts of me, parts I wouldn't want to miss.

I don't take for granted my friends and my family; they make up who I am, my heart, my sanity. I couldn't replace them; without them, I could not be. I could not take it; I wouldn't be the best of me.

I pass these traits onto 1, 2, 3, and 4, hoping they see the value more. We're connected through the blood, the bones, and I love you.

Triumph over Trauma

"My eyes wake with tears flowing,
Blanketing my face with a warm yet chilling
touch.
I remember what I saw last: you, standing there.
You reminded me of how much you hated who I
was,
Showing me the worst of you just because I
wasn't enough.
But neither were you; this is what it's come to.

You get to be free while I'm trapped in my head,
Remembering all the things you did and said.
Recalling the fights because you hated me so
much,
Reminding myself of how every swing was a
bad touch.
You broke me down and tore me apart,
And for what? So you could feel like you left
your mark?

You get to be free, but not me; no matter what, I
can't get away,
Even though you're not here. I live less scared
but still in fear,
Fear that you'd return or I'd see you somewhere.

And once again, I'd be just as scared.

You don't know what's waiting if you come
back,
You don't know that my fear will fuel the fire to
my pack.
You would see just what you'd get in return; it'd
be so sweet, it's true.

I have an army now, and you'd lose; this I
promise you."

Unyielding Resolve

It's not easy
When I don't know what the future holds,
All I can do is be filled with hope
That I won't lose my believers cloak.

I know my soul is safe,
Guided by spirits.
I know which way is the way,
I know because I'm in it.

I refuse to be lost in this sea of unpleasantry,
I have too much at stake, the plans to make,
The things I'm doing presently.

I will not fall short,
Nor will I ever run.
I will always try from moon up to down sun.

Beyond Never

It's on the other side of never that you'll find the
side of me,
The side that perseveres,
The side of me that's free to be.

I waited longer than what feels like forever,
To find my comfort and my truth,
I know who I am and I know what I can do.

I was stuck in a shell of lonely,
I lost myself a time or two,
But freedom is among myself,
My future is in view.

You can't tell me I don't try,
You can't stop my runner's high.
No more giving into hate,
It's my life, it's not too late.

I found comfort in my love,
I found solace and I found peace.
I have my friends and family,
They always save me, maybe not easily,
But always definitely.

From Street Lights to Responsibilities

Certainly! Here's the extended version:

When the street lights meant "get on home,"
And you had to share a landline phone.
Grandma always made sure you'd eat,
And you could walk outside in your bare feet.

The best part of free time meant outside,
Sometimes Sundays meant car rides.
The hugs were long, and the summers too short,
But for what it's worth,

We were happy.
We were healthy.
We had so much time to grow.
Fun was endless, timeless memories
Were shared, little did we know.

Other things we enjoyed in the 90s,
Full of simple joys and carefree sprees.

That one day we'd have families
And bills we had to pay.
Things to do and stuff to plan,
Like our parents did, back in our day.

Breaking Chains

Hey there, you,
Stuck with no escape in view.
Feeling like there's nothing good,
Nothing left for you.
You don't have to be afraid
Of taking a chance, you see.
You can get out, you can be free,
You just have to leave.

Don't stay because they "need" you,
Don't stay because of paper,
Lines with regret when feelings taper.
They aren't the same hands you once knew,
Now they're hurtful, hurtful to you.

It's not your fault they are
Broken love.
This isn't your problem,
They just aren't the one.
No need to be stuck in the worst way possible,
It's okay to run away from what feels
impossible.

Take a step towards a life that's serene,
Find peace, let your spirit intervene.

Craft a plan for solace, make it real,
Break free from the pain that you feel.

Remember, there's support out there,
Friends, professionals who genuinely care.
You deserve happiness, a life that's bright,
Take those steps, embrace the light.

Healing Journey

In this process, a freeing journey unfolds,
Wishing the best for you, as tales are told.

Your trauma does not define you,
Your trauma does not control
The depths of your being,
The peace of your soul.

Your heart is healing,
You'll soon have relief,
As long as you keep on trying,
As long as you believe.

Keep fighting for yourself,
Don't let the enemy win.
Take mental therapy,
Gain some clarity,
So you can feel again.

www.ingramcontent.com/pod-product-compliance
Lightning Source LLC
LaVergne TN
LVHW021330200726
843509LV00014B/2466